GALAXIES AND DEEP SPACE

Lisa Regan

PowerKiDS press

Published in 2021 by
The Rosen Publishing Group, Inc.
29 East 21st Street, New York, NY 10010

Cataloging-in-Publication Data

Names: Regan, Lisa.
Title: Galaxies and deep space / Lisa Regan.
Description: New York : PowerKids Press, 2021. | Series: Fact frenzy: space | Includes glossary and index.
Identifiers: ISBN 9781725320161 (pbk.) | ISBN 9781725320185 (library bound) | ISBN 9781725320178 (6 pack)
Subjects: LCSH: Galaxies--Juvenile literature. | Outer space--Juvenile literature.
Classification: LCC QB857.3 R465 2021 | DDC 523.1'12--dc23

Copyright © Arcturus Holdings Ltd, 2021

All rights reserved. No part of this book may be reproduced in any form without permission in writing from the publisher, except by a reviewer.

Manufactured in the United States of America

CPSIA Compliance Information: Batch CSPK20: For Further Information contact Rosen Publishing, New York, New York at 1-800-237-9932.

Contents

New planets are discovered almost every day page 6

and other facts about exoplanets

Some planets have two suns page 8

and other facts about circumbinary planets

Galaxies can eat each other page 10

and other facts about galaxies

The Rotten Egg Nebula smells terrible page 12

and other facts about nebulae

There may be up to 2 trillion galaxies page 14

and more facts about galaxies

A black hole could stretch you like spaghetti page 16

and other facts about black holes

A huge cloud of water floats through space page 18

and other facts about the universe's oldest cloud

There could be an infinite number of universes page 20

and other facts about the multiverse theory

We might have found aliens without realizing page 22

and other facts about alien life

95% of the universe is missing page 24

and other facts about dark matter

Even More Facts! page 26

Glossary page 28

Further Information page 31

Index page 32

FACT 1: NEW PLANETS ARE DISCOVERED ALMOST EVERY DAY

Back in 1994, scientists Michel Mayor and Didier Queloz found a planet outside our solar system—but people didn't believe them for almost a year! Now we have found thousands, with more discovered all the time.

Exoplanets

An exoplanet is what we call a planet outside our solar system. Exoplanets circle around other stars, just as Earth circles around the sun. Although no exoplanets were found until the 1990s, scientists had believed for years before this time that they existed. The reason behind this belief was that in understanding how planets formed around our sun, scientists realized that planets would similarly form around other sun-like stars.

An artist's impression of 51 Pegasi b circling a star.

Too big

So if scientists believed in exoplanets, why did it take them so long to be convinced by the two scientists' 1994 discovery? Well, the issue was that this planet, named 51 Pegasi b—the first ever found circling around a sun-like star—was just too big. The existence of an exoplanet this size didn't fit with scientists' ideas at the time about how planets were formed, so they thought at first that it must be a mistake.

I'm looking for a Goldilocks planet!

Goldilocks planets

The powerful telescopes available today help with spotting exoplanets. One focus of this search is finding "Goldilocks planets," named after the fairy tale. Like Goldilocks searching through the bears' house, scientists are trying to find a planet that is not too hot, not too cold, but just right for life to exist there.

Not the first

51 Pegasi b was the first exoplanet to be discovered orbiting a sun-like star, but it was not the first exoplanet to be discovered. In 1992, Aleksander Wolszczan and Dale Frail found exoplanets around a type of tiny, fast-spinning star called a pulsar, which is the squeezed core left over after a massive star explodes.

FACT 2 The first evidence of an exoplanet was noted in 1917 ... but it was not recognized as a planet at the time.

FACT 3: SOME PLANETS HAVE TWO SUNS

More than half of all star systems in the known universe circle around two stars rather than one. Can you imagine having a second sun in the sky?

FACT 4
Scientists have found planets with three suns, and one giant planet with four suns.

Strange as fiction
Our solar system has one sun, but more than half of all solar systems in the known universe circle around two stars. Planets that circle around two stars are officially called "circumbinary planets," but sometimes they are also known as "Tatooine planets"—after Luke Skywalker's home planet in *Star Wars*, which famously has two suns.

Two suns? At least I remembered enough sunglasses!

Changing journeys

We move regularly around the sun—one journey all the way around takes 365 (and ¼) days, an Earth year. (We have a leap year every four years to make up the quarter-days.) But for planets with more than one sun, it isn't so simple. Their movement is much more irregular and their journey time—and sometimes even their path—around their suns varies.

Hard to find

The Kepler space observatory, which looks for Earth-size planets orbiting other stars, has found a number of planets with two suns. But it's not easy—because of their irregular movement, scientists find it quite tricky to spot these planets. They search for small dips in a star's brightness, as these suggest that a planet could be passing in front of it and blocking a little bit of its light.

In the Kepler-47 system, two planets move around two suns.

Rare planets

Although most star systems have more than one star, it is quite rare for a two-star system to have any planets moving around it. The Kepler space observatory has found 2,600 planets beyond our solar system, but only 11 of them circle around more than one star. Scientists think that the magnetic force of the stars may hurl planets away from them, out of orbit.

The Kepler telescope was launched into space aboard a rocket in 2009.

FACT 5
GALAXIES CAN EAT EACH OTHER

Big galaxies crash into each other every 9 billion years or so. When this happens, they sometimes swallow up and merge with the other galaxy in order to grow larger. They're space cannibals!

Get your own gas!

Gas it up
Galaxies need lots of gas to make new stars. Smaller galaxies have plenty of gas for this, but bigger galaxies are often running uncomfortably low. By merging with smaller galaxies, these bigger galaxies can be sure that their gas levels are full and that they will be able to continue making new stars.

These two galaxies, known as "The Mice" because of their long tails, are in the process of merging.

The Milky Way

Our galaxy, the Milky Way, has already eaten 15 smaller galaxies—chomp! It is likely to eat another two small galaxies, the Large and Small Magellanic Clouds, within 4 billion years or so. The Milky Way is in a stage of its life as a galaxy where it is now easier to keep itself going by swallowing up other galaxies than by creating its own stars.

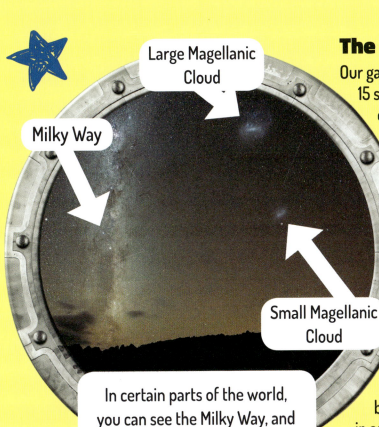

Large Magellanic Cloud

Milky Way

Small Magellanic Cloud

In certain parts of the world, you can see the Milky Way, and the Large and Small Magellanic Clouds in the night sky.

Big bad Andromeda?

But the Milky Way might not be at the top of the galaxy food chain ... Some scientists think that our galaxy will itself be swallowed up by the Andromeda galaxy in around 5 billion years. It depends on how big Andromeda really is—for a long time it was believed to be around twice the size of the Milky Way, but a recent study has found that it might actually be the same size.

Merging stars

It isn't only galaxies that crash into each other and merge into one. Stars do it too, with a "stellar collision" of this type happening somewhere in the universe once every 10,000 years. All types of stars can merge—one particularly strange mix is a Thorne-Żytkow object, where a neutron star and a red giant star crash and merge. What you get is a neutron star in the middle, surrounded by a red giant!

An artist's impression of two neutron stars merging.

FACT 6: THE ROTTEN EGG NEBULA SMELLS TERRIBLE

What's in a name? Well, for the Rotten Egg Nebula there's quite a bit of truth to it. It contains a lot of sulfur, which when combined with other materials smells like rotten eggs!

Gross!

What is a nebula?

A nebula (plural nebulae) is an enormous cloud of dust and gas in space. Some nebulae are areas where new stars are starting to form, and others are the remains flung out into space by a dying star. Either way, they exist in what we call interstellar space—areas of space in between star systems.

Faraway stink

Don't worry too much about catching a whiff of this space stinker—it's far enough from Earth that we can't smell it at all. The Rotten Egg Nebula is about 5,000 light years from Earth, meaning that it's so far away it takes light 5,000 years to travel that far. To give an idea of how far away that is, it takes light less than 1.5 seconds to travel between Earth and the Moon.

Big change

The Rotten Egg Nebula is interesting to scientists because it's going through a change that they are rarely able to see happening. A red giant star is in the process of dying, and violently shedding its outer layers of gas and dust. This change takes around 2,000 years in total, which sounds like a long time but is a blink of an eye in space terms, so it's lucky for scientists to see it in action.

The Hubble telescope took this picture of the Horsehead Nebula.

THE WORD "NEBULA" COMES FROM THE LATIN WORD FOR "CLOUD."

The Witch Head Nebula looks like a witch screaming into space—scary stuff!

Nebula names

The Rotten Egg Nebula does actually have a more polite name—it's also known as the Calabash Nebula. A calabash is a kind of vegetable that has a shape a bit like a bowling pin, which is sort of what this nebula looks like. Other nebulae have names that describe what they look like, too—some of the spookiest are the Ghost, Skull, and Witch Head nebulae!

FACT 7

THERE MAY BE UP TO 2 TRILLION GALAXIES

Scientists find it hard to agree on how many galaxies there are in the universe. Some think it's 200 million, a computer program said 500 million, and others believe there are far, far more.

The big questions

When scientists try to work out the answers to huge questions about space, such as "How many galaxies are there in the known universe?", they have to use the information that people have already gathered and use it to make predictions. Computer programs now help scientists to do this in more complex and accurate ways than were possible in the past.

It's out of this world, man!

Computers are a huge part of space science, from controlling missions to running simulations with data.

Seen and unseen

Scientists got to the figure of 2 trillion galaxies by creating models in a computer program, based on the Hubble telescope's 20-year collection of images. The Hubble telescope shows us more of space than ever, but scientists believe that only 10% of the known universe's galaxies are visible to us now. The figure of 2 trillion galaxies takes this into account, so it's a lot higher than the number of galaxies that have actually been seen.

Galaxy shapes

The galaxies that we can see at the moment don't all look the same. Most are in the shape of a spiral or an egg, but some have no particular shape at all—they just look like a vague assortment of stars, gas, and dust spread out in all directions. Our galaxy, the Milky Way, is a spiral galaxy.

Sombreros and tadpoles

Scientists have had great fun naming some of the galaxies that we've discovered so far. There is the Sombrero Galaxy, the Tadpole Galaxy, and the Sunflower Galaxy, for starters. The Milky Way's name comes from an ancient Greek myth about the goddess Hera spraying milk across the sky. In China, it is called the Silver River, and in the Kalahari Desert in southern Africa it is known as the Backbone of Night.

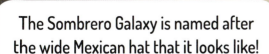

The Sombrero Galaxy is named after the wide Mexican hat that it looks like!

FACT 8: A BLACK HOLE COULD STRETCH YOU LIKE SPAGHETTI

Don't get too close to the edge of a black hole! If it's a smallish one, its gravity will pull hardest on the closest part of you and streeeeetch it away from the rest.

Spaghettification

This all sounds terrifying, but at least it gives us a great word—spaghettification! This describes how an object falling into a black hole is stretched, and sometimes ripped apart, by the force of gravity. An object spaghettified by a black hole would be trapped inside it, stretching out farther and farther forever and ever.

It's one way to grow taller!

FACT 9

White holes, the opposite of black holes, should be possible, but we haven't found any yet. They would only give out light and matter, nothing would be able to enter them.

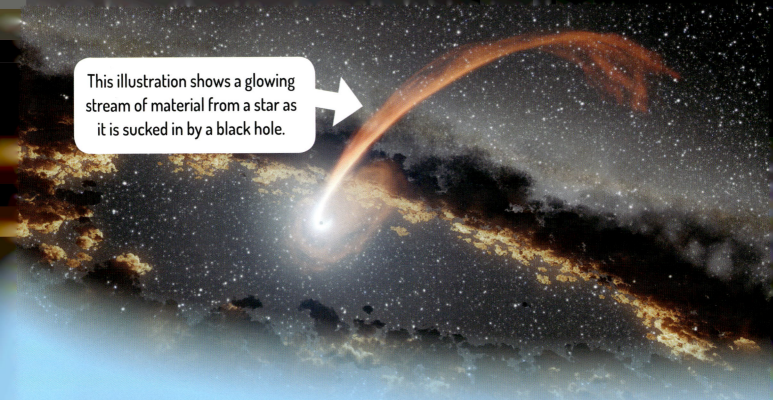

This illustration shows a glowing stream of material from a star as it is sucked in by a black hole.

No escape

A black hole has very strong gravity, which gets much stronger the closer you get to it. Once you have been sucked into the black hole, you can't escape it—no matter or light can. That's why black holes are invisible.

Spaghettifying stars

It's not just humans who are at risk of this spaghettification—we know that it happens to stars. In fact, we've seen black holes tearing stars apart in this way! Stars are only at risk if they stray too close to the edge of a black hole, though. This is called the black hole's "event horizon," and it's like the edge of a waterfall—the closest anything can get without being pulled down into it.

Exploring a black hole

There may be no escape from a black hole, but if you'd like to at least be able to have a look around inside rather than be totally spaghettified, make sure to pick a big one. The gravity of very large black holes is enough to suck you in whole. Most galaxies have the largest type of black hole—our galaxy, the Milky Way, has one called Sagittarius A in its middle.

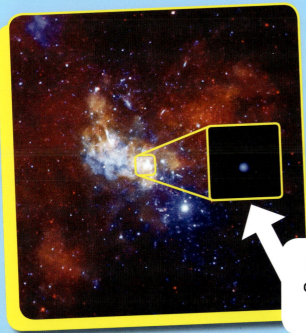

Scientists think this blue dot was a flash of light, caused when an asteroid fell into Sagittarius A and was torn apart.

17

FACT 10 — A HUGE CLOUD OF WATER FLOATS THROUGH SPACE

Scientists have found a cloud far off in outer space that holds 140 trillion times the amount of water in the Earth's oceans. It is the biggest amount of water that we have identified.

How much?

So, 140 trillion is such a huge number that it's hard to even imagine how big it really is. Think about it this way—if you counted out 140 trillion seconds, it would take more than 4 million years! Our galaxy, the Milky Way, has a few large clouds of water, but this giant is around 4,000 times bigger than any of them.

I feel so small ...

FACT 11 — Most of the water in our galaxy is in the form of ice.

Old water

Scientists believe that this area of water is around 12 billion years old—to give an idea of just how old that really is, the universe only came into existence around 13.8 billion years ago. This means that water was one of the first materials ever created. Before the cloud's discovery, scientists thought that water was first created around a billion years after we now know it was.

Black hole

As if being a universe-wide record breaker for holding water wasn't dramatic enough, this giant cloud also surrounds a huge black hole! This black hole has 20 billion times the mass of the sun and it is part of a strange, giant object called a quasar, which gives out a huge amount of energy.

Finding the cloud

This cloud is so far away from Earth that it has taken light from where it is in space around 12 billion years to reach us. Light travels faster than anything else in the known universe, so that's a pretty long way away! Amazingly, we have developed such powerful telescopes that scientists were able to discover the cloud using two of them in Hawaii and California.

This telescope in Hawaii has a pretty beautiful view of Earth, too!

FACT 12

THERE COULD BE AN INFINITE NUMBER OF UNIVERSES

Some of the most cutting-edge ideas about space can sound like something out of science fiction. To make sense of the strangeness of space, scientists have to open their minds to all sorts of possibilities.

Rules don't apply

Scientists are learning more about space every day, but sometimes instead of this answering any big questions, it just raises many more new questions! We know that lots of things about space don't fit in exactly with our rules for how things work on Earth, so scientists have to think creatively about the different models that could make our universe work the way it seems to.

Not alone?

One of the most out-there ideas about our universe is simply that it's not the only one. Most scientists until now have worked on the assumption that nothing else exists beyond or alongside our universe—that our universe is literally everything. But until around 100 years ago, we thought that our galaxy was the only one in existence, whereas now we know it's just one of billions upon billions ...

Multiverse theory

The idea that there is more than one universe is known as the "multiverse" theory. Within this idea, there are lots of possibilities for how these multiple universes might be arranged. Some scientists have thought about them as bubbles within bubbles, some as a patchwork quilt stretching on forever, some as slices of bread side by side within a larger loaf.

Could our universe be just one patch in the quilt of existence?

That's a lot of universes!

Infinite universes

If we describe something as infinite, it means it is never-ending. One version of the multiverse theory is that there are infinite universes. This is based on the understanding that there is no limit to how much space and time exists—in this case, why would we be limited to one universe, or any number of universes? These other universes may be invisible to us, but that doesn't necessarily mean they don't exist. Strange to think about!

FACT 13: WE MIGHT HAVE FOUND ALIENS WITHOUT REALIZING

One of the biggest questions about the universe is "Are we alone?" The answer? We still don't know. Scientists don't think they've found alien life, but they admit they might not recognize it if they saw it.

Seeing in space

It can be tricky for scientists to see exactly what's going on far off in space. When things are very distant from Earth, it's not like looking at something through binoculars on Earth. They can't always get a clear, detailed picture of what they're trying to see, so it might be tricky to see signs of life. Sometimes scientists can't actually "see" an object at all, but they know it's there from how it affects its surroundings.

Hey ... HEY ... I'm over here!

NASA IS CURRENTLY RUNNING MISSIONS TO TRY TO FIND ALIEN LIFE IN SPACE.

Unfamiliar beings

It can be hard to imagine something completely outside your own experiences. When scientists look for proof of life elsewhere in the universe, they are searching for evidence based on their knowledge of the needs and qualities of living things on Earth. But alien life might be so different from any sort of life we're familiar with that scientists are missing the very different signs of its existence.

Simple life

When we imagine alien life, we often think of creatures fairly similar to ourselves—they may look different, they might be bright green with huge pulsating brains, but they are intelligent life-forms. Actually, many planets and moons may be able to support some kind of simple life, like the bacteria we have on Earth, but the chances of finding intelligent life is far lower.

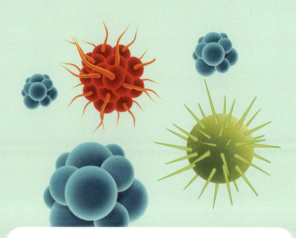

Alien life may be simple, tiny creatures like bacteria—or something else entirely!

Extreme Earth

Scientists have found living creatures surviving in conditions on Earth so extreme that we thought it was impossible for any life to exist there. They have discovered simple life-forms called microbes living in burning-hot pure acid in Ethiopia's Danakil Depression, one of the hottest places on Earth. Studying these extreme-living microbes helps us understand how and where alien life might be found in space, in conditions where humans couldn't survive.

The Danakil Depression might look like somewhere on another planet, but it's right here on Earth!

23

FACT 14
95% OF THE UNIVERSE IS MISSING

Less than 5% of the universe is made of matter and energy as we understand it and can see it. The rest of it is invisible dark matter and dark energy. Gulp.

Missing matter

Scientists have realized that in space, lots of things aren't quite adding up ... For instance, galaxies are spinning so quickly that the gravity from their visible matter shouldn't be strong enough to hold them together. They should have torn themselves apart a long time ago, but they haven't. Scientists think this is because they have more matter, which is invisible to us—they call this dark matter.

95% Dark matter

5% Atomic matter

Spinning so quickly means we have to hold on tight!

Dark energy

Dark energy is even more mysterious than dark matter—and scientists think it makes up over 70% of the universe. While scientists have some ideas about what dark matter might be—strange and not-yet-seen particles—they struggle a lot more to explain dark energy. The reason they think it exists is because the universe is growing and pulling galaxies farther apart, so there must be a greater force acting against the gravity that holds galaxies together.

Astronomical voids

There are huge areas in space where there are no or very few galaxies—scientists call them astronomical voids. But what looks like empty space to us might be something that we just don't understand yet. There is a giant Cold Spot in the universe, a cooler area that scientists think has many of these voids, and one idea is that it could be the spot where our universe crashed into another one!

Still learning

Essentially, dark matter and dark energy are what scientists think bridge the gap between what we have measured in space and how we see the universe behaving. We are still only just starting to understand many things about space, and how its strange forces and structures work. Many ideas that scientists have today might turn out to be wrong, or to be only one part of the answer—that's how science develops.

EVEN MORE FACTS!

You've found out lots about galaxies and deep space, but there's always more to discover! Boost your knowledge here with even more facts.

In 1543, the Polish astronomer Nicolaus Copernicus published a book claiming that Earth and the planets orbited the sun. Before this, people believed that the sun and planets orbited Earth.

The Hubble Space Telescope was launched into space in 1990. It was named after Edwin Hubble, an American astronomer who, in 1929, noticed that the furthest galaxies were moving faster than those closer to us.

In October 1995, 51 Pegasi b, or "51 Peg," was the first planet to be discovered circling a sun-like star. It is 50 light-years from Earth, has a temperature of 1,800 °F (1,000 °C), and orbits its host star every 4 days.

Within the first four years of Kepler Space Telescope's launch in 2009, it had detected 2,000 exoplanets belonging to individual stars. There are now more than 3,200 confirmed exoplanets.

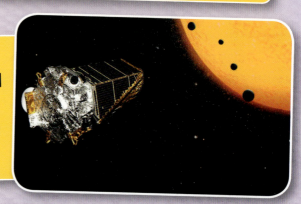

It has been estimated that there is at least one exoplanet circling every star in the galaxy, which means there are approximately a trillion exoplanets in our galaxy, many of them the size of Earth.

The first designs for the Kepler Space Telescope, proposed by William Borucki of the NASA Ames Research Center, were rejected by NASA four times in the 1990s before finally being approved in 2001.

The sun is just one of over 300 billion stars in the Milky Way galaxy. Scientists estimate that there are 2 trillion galaxies in the universe, including those that have not yet been seen.

The Large Magellanic Cloud is a satellite galaxy that orbits the Milky Way. It is about 163,000 light-years away and around one-hundredth the size of the Milky Way. Some scientists think that the Milky Way is pulling and warping the shape of it.

The closest known nebula to Earth is called the Helix Nebula. It is approximately 700 light-years away from Earth, which means if you could travel at the speed of light, it would still take you 700 years to get there!

The closest galaxy to the Milky Way is the Andromeda galaxy, which is about 2.6 million light-years away from us.

GALAXIES AND DEEP SPACE GLOSSARY

asteroid A small, rocky object made up of material left over from the birth of the solar system.

astronomer A scientist who studies the stars, planets, and other natural objects in space.

astronomical void A vast area of space containing very few galaxies or none at all.

Big Bang The way in which many scientists believe the universe began—a huge, hot explosion that expanded out all the matter in the universe from one tiny point. Since this explosion, the universe has continued growing outward and is still doing so today.

black hole A superdense point in space, usually formed by a collapsed core of a giant star. A black hole's gravity is so powerful that even light cannot escape from it.

core The central part of something.

dark energy An unknown form of energy that many scientists think exists throughout the universe, acting in opposition to gravity, and causing the universe to expand faster and faster over time.

Earth day The 24 hours it takes for Earth to make one complete rotation on its axis.

exoplanet A planet orbiting a star outside our solar system.

galaxy A large system of stars, gas, and dust with anything from millions to trillions of stars.

gravity A natural force created around objects with mass, which draws other objects toward them.

light-year The distance light travels in a year—about 5.9 trillion miles (9.5 trillion km).

mass The amount of physical matter in an object.

Milky Way Our home galaxy, a spiral with a bar across its core. Our solar system is about 28,000 light-years from the monster black hole at its heart.

moon Earth's closest companion in space, a ball of rock that orbits Earth every 27.3 Earth days. Most other planets in the solar system have moons of their own.

NASA An abbreviation for "National Aeronautics and Space Administration," the American government organization concerned with spacecraft and space travel.

nebula A cloud of gas or dust floating in space. Nebulae are the raw material used to make stars.

neutron star The core of a supermassive star, left behind by a supernova explosion and collapsed to the size of a city. Many neutron stars are also pulsars.

observatory A building or room that contains a telescope or other scientific equipment used to study space.

orbit A fixed path taken by one object in space around another because of the effect of gravity.

planet A world, orbiting a star, that has enough mass and gravity to pull itself into a ball-like shape, and clear space around it of other large objects.

pulsar A fast-spinning neutron star whose intense magnetic field forces its radiation into two narrow beams, which sweep around the sky like a lighthouse. From Earth, a pulsar appears as a quickly flashing star.

GALAXIES AND DEEP SPACE GLOSSARY continued

quasar A distant, active object in space that has a very bright core and gives out a huge amount of energy.

satellite Any object orbiting a planet. Moons are natural satellites made of rock and ice. Artificial satellites are machines in orbit around Earth.

solar system The eight planets (including Earth) and their moons, and other objects such as asteroids, that orbit around the Sun.

spacecraft A vehicle that travels into space.

spiral galaxy A galaxy with a hub of old yellow stars (sometimes crossed by a bar) surrounded by a flattened disc of younger stars, gas, and dust. Bright, newborn stars make a spiral pattern across the disc.

telescope A device that collects light or other radiations from space and uses them to create a bright, clear image. Telescopes can use either a lens or a mirror to collect light.

universe The whole of space including all the galaxies, solar systems, stars, and the planets.

FURTHER INFORMATION

BOOKS

Aguilar, David. *Space Encyclopedia*. London, UK: National Geographic Kids, 2013.

Becklade, Sue. *Wild About Space*. Thaxted, UK: Miles Kelly, 2020.

Betts, Bruce. *Astronomy for Kids: How to Explore Outer Space with Binoculars, a Telescope, or Just Your Eyes!* Emeryville, CA: Rockridge Press, 2018.

DK. *The Astronomy Book: Big Ideas Simply Explained*. London, UK: DK, 2017.

DK. *Knowledge Encyclopedia Space!: The Universe as You've Never Seen It Before*. London, UK: DK, 2015.

Frith, Alex, Jerome Martin, and Alice James. *100 Things to Know About Space*. London, UK: Usborne Publishing, 2016.

National Geographic Kids. *Everything: Space. London*, UK: Collins, 2018.

WEBSITES

Ducksters Astronomy for Kids
http://www.ducksters.com/science/astronomy.php
Head to this website to find out all there is to know about astronomy; you can also try an astronomy crossword puzzle and word search!

NASA Science: Space Place
https://spaceplace.nasa.gov
Discover all sorts of facts about space, other planets, and the moon. You can even play the Mars Rover Game, sending commands to the Mars rover and collecting as much data as possible in eight expeditions!

Science Kids: Space for Kids
http://www.sciencekids.co.nz/space.html
Go beyond our planet and explore space through fun facts, games, videos, quizzes, and projects.

Publisher's note to educators and parents: Our editors have carefully reviewed these websites to ensure that they are suitable for students. Many websites change frequently, however, and we cannot guarantee that a site's future contents will continue to meet our high standards of quality and educational value. Be advised that students should be closely supervised whenever they access the Internet.

INDEX

A
aliens 22–23
Andromeda 11, 27
asteroids 17
astronomers 26
astronomical voids 25

B
bacteria 23
black holes 16–17, 19
Borucki, William 27

C
Calabash Nebula 12, 13
circumbinary planets 8
Copernicus, Nicolaus 26
crashes 10, 11, 25

D
Danakil Depression 23
dark energy 24, 25
dark matter 24, 25

E
Earth years 9
exoplanets 6–7, 8–9, 26

F
Frail, Dale 7

G
galaxies 10–11, 14–15, 17, 18, 21, 24, 26, 27
gas 10, 12
gravity 16, 17, 24, 25

H
Hawaii 19
Helix Nebula 27
Horsehead Nebula 13
Hubble, Edwin 26
Hubble Space Telescope 13, 15, 26

I
ice 18
interstellar space 12

K
Kepler-47 system 9
Kepler space observatory 9
Kepler Space Telescope 9, 26, 27

L
Large Magellanic Cloud 11, 27
light 9, 13, 17, 19, 27
light-years 13, 26

M
Mayor, Michel 6
Mice galaxies 10
microbes 23
Milky Way 11, 15, 17, 18, 27
moons 23
multiverse theory 21

N
NASA 23, 27
nebulae 12–13, 27
neutron stars 11

P
pulsars 7

Q
quasars 19
Queloz, Didier 6

R
red giant stars 11, 13
Rotten Egg Nebula 12, 13

S
Sagittarius A 17
Small Magellanic Cloud 11
solar system 6, 8
Sombrero Galaxy 15
spaghettification 16–17
spiral galaxies 15
stars 6, 7, 8–9, 10, 11, 12, 13, 17, 26, 27
star systems 8, 9, 12
sulfur 12
sun 6, 7, 8, 9, 27
suns 8, 9

T
telescopes 7, 9, 13, 15, 19
Thorne-Zytkow 11

U
universes 20–21, 24, 25

W
white holes 16
Witch Head Nebula 13
Wolszczan, Aleksander 7